Visiting the Past

Auschwitz

Jane Shuter

Heinemann Library
Chicago, Illinois

Designed by Visual Image
Illustrations by Visual Image
Printed in Hong Kong

04 03 02 01 00
10 9 8 7 6 5 4 3 2 1

Library of Congress Cataloging-in-Publication Data
Shuter, Jane
        Auschwitz / Jane Shuter
            p. cm. – (Visiting the past)
        Includes bibliographical references and index.
        Summary: Discusses the purpose, processing of inmates, daily life,
    and other activities and aspects of the Nazi concentration camps
    Auschwitz and Birkenau.
        ISBN 1-57572-856-7
        1. Auschwitz (Concentration camp) Juvenile literature.
    2. Birkenau (Concentration camp) Juvenile literature. 3. Holocaust,
    Jewish (1939-1945) Juvenile literature. [1. Auschwitz
    (Concentration camp) 2. Birkenau (Concentration camp)
    3. Concentration camps—Poland. 4. Holocaust, Jewish (1939-1945)]
    I. Title. II. Series.
    D805.5.A96S58 1999
    940.53'18'094386—dc21   99-14227
                                                          CIP

Acknowledgments
The Publishers would like to thank Emma Robertson and Magnet Harlequin for permission to
reproduce all photographs, apart from those on pages 7 (bottom), 10 (bottom) and 16, which
are reproduced with permission of the Panstwowe Muzeum Oswiecim [Auschwitz State
Museum].

Cover photograph reproduced with permission of AKG London.

Every effort has been made to contact copyright holders of any material reproduced in this
book. Any omissions will be rectified in subsequent printings if notice is given to the publisher.

Some words are shown in bold, **like this**. You can find out what they
mean by looking in the glossary.

Contents

The Nazi Period

Auschwitz was one of many **concentration camps** set up by the **Nazis** in the 1940s during the Second World War. People imprisoned here died from starvation, overwork, and ill-treatment. Many more were sent here simply to be killed. People visit Auschwitz today to remember those who died. But why did the Nazis set up camps like this?

Division and persecution

The Nazi Party (National Socialist German Workers Party), led by Adolf Hitler, came to power in Germany in 1933. The Nazis wanted Germany to be powerful. They also wanted only **Aryan** people living there: blonde, blue-eyed, and healthy, with "pure" German blood. People who did not fit this image were "undesirables"—such as the disabled, black people, gypsies, homosexuals, and, most of all, Jews.

The Nazis produced made-up **statistics** to blame the Jews for everything from Germany's loss of the First World War to the economic crisis in Germany. Children were taught in school that, while Germany was suffering high levels of **unemployment** and poverty, all Jews were well off. The Nazis passed laws against Jews, stopping them from working and living where they wanted, and taking away other **rights**. They put their political opponents and other "undesirables" into concentration camps.

The main gate of Auschwitz I. The words across the top say "*Arbeit Macht Frei*" ("Work will set you free"). It underlines the idea that the camps were set up to provide the Nazis with a pool of forced labor.

4

Auschwitz camp was set up in 1940, in Nazi-occupied Poland, on the site of some former Polish army **barracks**. At first it held **political prisoners**, mostly Polish. Later it was used for captured **Soviet** soldiers and Jews.

From the day the camp was set up until the Nazis left in 1945, the Nazis called Auschwitz, as well as the camps that grew up around it, work camps. But the main purpose of the camps was not to provide a healthy, efficient group of workers. If so, the Nazis would have fed their prisoners more, worked them less hard, and provided them with tools and equipment. The main purpose of these camps was to imprison, and later to murder, those who opposed the government, or whom the Nazis chose to **persecute** for racial reasons, such as Jews.

There were two rows of barbed-wire fences, with **guardhouses** set all along them. Prisoners were not supposed to go near the fence. Survivors of the camp say that some guards deliberately threw prisoners' caps close to the fence and sent them to fetch the caps—knowing the prisoners would be shot for approaching the fence.

Fences and barbed wire shut off each **compound** of Auschwitz II (also called Birkenau camp) from the other compounds, the **crematoria** (in the woods at the end), the main paths, and the railway line.

The barbed wire was electrified. Survivors of the camp say that many people chose deliberately to run at the fences to commit suicide. They were either shot by the guards or electrified on the fence.

How Auschwitz Changed

Auschwitz was first planned to hold up to 10,000 people. Between 1940 and 1943, the camp grew and grew. The first camp, based on the Polish **barracks**, became Auschwitz I. A second, far larger camp called Auschwitz II was built nearby at Birkenau. The promise of cheap labor tempted various industries to set up factories in the area, built by prisoners from Auschwitz. By 1944, there were about 40 small camps within a few miles, providing workers for these industries. The combined camps held hundreds of thousands of people. But millions of people had been sent there. Most died there.

In 1941, the first mass **gassing** of prisoners was held at Auschwitz—600 **Soviet** prisoners of war and 250 patients sick with tuberculosis—an infectious lung disease. From then on, more and more people were gassed. Special **gas chambers** were built in which to kill them, along with **crematoria** to burn their bodies. Special death camps were set up, mainly for killing Jews. Birkenau became Auschwitz's death camp. At first, when a trainload of Jews reached Birkenau, selections were carried out. The old, the very young, and the sick were weeded out for immediate death. Strong young men were kept to work. After 1944, selections were made less often. Everyone went straight to the gas chambers.

This is the main gate at Birkenau

Birkenau is much bigger than Auschwitz I. The camp stretches as far as a person can see, even from the top of the main guard tower.

Destroying the evidence

When the **Nazis** saw that they might lose the war, they tried to cover up exactly what had been going on in the camps, especially the death camps. In January 1945, with the Soviet army closing in on Auschwitz, the Nazis began to burn piles of official papers, blow up the gas chambers, and destroy other evidence. But the Soviets advanced too quickly. The Nazis were forced to flee, herding as many prisoners as could walk to camps deeper in German territory. Many of those who were too sick to walk were shot, but there was not time to shoot them all.

The Soviets arrived at 3 P.M. on January 27, 1945, and found 7,600 survivors in Auschwitz and its other camps. The truth about the death camps emerged. People could see the bodies of prisoners, look at the partially destroyed records, and, most importantly, they could talk to the survivors. The evidence of survivors is vital for a reconstruction of life in Auschwitz and for an understanding of the site today. Any information that we have been given that does not come directly from the site comes from the records or survivors' stories.

Here is a line of mostly women and children, being marched to the gas chambers. Those being taken to the gas chambers were told that they were going to have a shower after their long journey. The picture above shows the site today.

7

Hard Labor

This book will, for the most part, look at living conditions in Auschwitz I and Birkenau. Many buildings remain, but these cannot show the people crammed into them. Nor can they show the daily ill-treatment by the guards, the savaging by guard dogs, the regular killing for any reason, or for no reason at all. This page and the next briefly describe some parts of prisoners' lives that the site cannot show, drawn from the **testimonies** of survivors.

This yard was used for executions. People were stood against the far wall and shot. The barred windows on the right are the windows of the prison block. The block on the left had shutters to stop the people in Block 10 (where medical experiments were carried out) from seeing out into the yard.

New arrivals at Auschwitz spent four weeks in **quarantine,** supposedly to stop the newcomers from bringing infections into the camp. In fact, it was to terrorize them into good behavior. They learned that they were just numbers, not people with names, that they had no rights at all in the eyes of the **Nazis**. They spent hours standing on **roll call** and were expected to obey orders given in German, whether they understood the language or not. They had to learn fast—those who did not were beaten brutally, even to death.

People who survived quarantine were organized into work groups. From then on, they worked from dawn to dusk, sometimes even longer. Prisoners who did the hardest outdoor work always ended the day by carrying home those who had died that day. Work groups were changed regularly. The **SS** (*Schutzstaffel*—the Nazi soldiers who controlled the camps) thought that a combination of the high death rate and constant shifting around would stop prisoners from forming **resistance** groups. It didn't, but it did make it harder for them to agree to resist, as did the Nazi practice of setting groups of prisoners against each other and making certain privileged prisoners **Blockältesters**—the officials in charge of each block.

A prison within a prison

Block 11 in Auschwitz I was the prison block. It dealt with "crimes" by Auschwitz inmates, such as not working hard enough or trying to escape. It also punished local people, such as those who formed resistance groups or who tried to help the prisoners, such as by giving them food as they went to and from the camps. Block 11 had ordinary prison cells, standing cells for more severe punishment, and an execution yard. Punishments included beatings, death by starvation in the cells, being sent to penal colonies—special work camps where prisoners were worked to death—and execution.

The only light and air for the ordinary cells came through this vent opening into the execution yard (below).

Standing cells were so small that prisoners could only stand in them. As many as four prisoners might be crammed into a space less than 3 feet (1 meter) square. They had no light, and their only air came in through the vents pictured above. Vents could become blocked by snow.

Processing People

Most prisoners arrived at Auschwitz and Birkenau by rail, in cattle cars, with about 80 people crammed in each car. **SS** officers herded them onto the platforms in a loud rush, meant to scare and confuse them. What happened next varied, depending on who the new arrivals were and where they were.

Political prisoners arriving at Auschwitz I would go straight to be recorded and put to work, after unloading those who had died on the journey. At Birkenau, especially with transports of Jews, there was often a selection made right on the platform, sorting out those fit enough to work from the old, the sick, and children.

Few people guessed what selection meant —they thought the fit and healthy were being chosen for harder work. In fact, the old, the sick, and most women and children were weeded out as useless. They were led off to their deaths. Only about 20 out of every 100 people who went through selection were selected for work and so entered the records of the camp.

The selection platform at Birkenau now, and in a photo taken by SS officials just after a train had been unloaded. The men have been separated from the women and children. The selection process happens next.

From names into numbers

Once selected, the process of turning people from human beings into numbers began. New arrivals had to take off all their clothes and put them, along with any other possessions, into paper bags. Then all the hair was shaved off their bodies, usually with a blunt razor, which was painful. They were sent into a huge shower room to wash, but the water was often deliberately too hot or too cold.

After this, they were given their prison uniforms. Finally, a clerk—who might also be a prisoner—filled in a form with their personal details and gave each one a number. The numbers were sewn onto their uniforms, replacing their names. From 1941 onward, many prisoners had their numbers tattooed on their left forearm. Auschwitz was the only camp where this was done, to help keep track of people, especially the bodies. Often, hundreds of people were killed in a single day.

Until 1943, all but the Jewish prisoners, who seldom entered the records at all because they were expected to die quickly, were photographed for the records. After 1943, photos were often not made.

Some of the uniforms that the prisoners wore. Clothes and shoes were handed out with no attention to whether they fitted.

Auschwitz I: Barracks

Most of the **barracks** in Auschwitz I were single-story brick buildings. They had several rooms leading off a wide central corridor that was used for serving meals and assembling prisoners. Several hundred prisoners were crammed into each block, or building, depending on the number of people in the camp. Later, another floor level was added to each barrack block. Each two-story block could hold more than 1,000 prisoners. By 1943, coal-burning stoves had been built into most blocks, although they were not lit regularly.

Tadeusz Iwaskzo, of the Auschwitz-Birkenau State Museum, has calculated that each prisoner had, on average, 88 cubic feet (2.5 cubic meters) of sleeping space. When people became too overcrowded, even by **Nazi** standards, wooden stable-type buildings were built between the brick blocks. Because they were supposed to be temporary, these had no heating and only mud floors.

The difference in the color of the bricks on this barrack block in Auschwitz I shows clearly where the second story was added.

The prisoner in charge of the block (the **Blockältester**) had his own room and was much more comfortable than the other prisoners. He could even collect a few possessions. But he was still a prisoner, and his position of power depended on him keeping in favor with the **SS**.

The first prisoners at Auschwitz I slept on straw on the floor.

Later, prisoners slept on straw mattresses, but these were packed together so tightly that the prisoners could sleep only on their sides.

Bunks were introduced in 1941, not for greater comfort, but so that three tiers of prisoners could be packed into a room. Depending on how full the camp was, there were at least two people to each bed.

The Blockältester had a private room.

Living in Auschwitz I

The first prisoners in Auschwitz I had no toilets or washrooms in their **barracks**, which were just bare sleeping spaces. The whole site had just two wells of cold spring water and one large **toilet pit** outside, with a wooden bar over it to balance on.

Washrooms and toilets were later built in each barrack block for the prisoners. There were 22 toilets to a two-story block. The washroom had 42 taps, and sometimes soap. Prisoners could use the toilets and washrooms only at certain times, usually first thing in the morning and last thing at night. Survivors say that prisoners who spent more than a minute at the washbasin were beaten, sometimes to death.

Here is a washroom and the toilet room in a block at Auschwitz I.

Food was served at the end of the corridor of each barrack block. It was cooked in the kitchen block, then taken to the barracks in barrels or big metal pots by the **Blockältester**. The **rations** had been carefully calculated to just keep the prisoners from starving to death. By the time the **SS** officials and the prisoners in charge of the blocks had helped themselves to the most nutritious foods, such as sausage and margarine, the 1,700 **calories** prisoners were supposed to be getting had fallen to 1,300 or even less.

A day's ration—at best

Breakfast 2 cups (500 ml) of coffee or tea. This was often nothing more than dried leaves or bark, usually birch, in hot water.

Midday 3 cups (750 ml) of thin turnip and potato soup, sometimes with other vegetables, a scrap of meat or Avo (a yeast extract) added.

Evening About 10 oz (300 g) of bread, less than an ounce of sausage or cheese, and a teaspoon each of margarine and beet jam.

The kitchen block of Auschwitz I provided food for the whole camp. By the time the food arrived at each block, it was usually cold. Prisoners who worked in the kitchen often took small amounts of food and fed them to people in the hospital blocks or to others who were close to death from starvation.

Birkenau BII: Wooden Huts

The wooden huts in Birkenau BII were originally designed as stables. There are still metal rings visible, three to a bay, for tying up horses. Each hut was designed to hold 54 horses but was converted to hold at least 400 people. Sometimes as many as 1,000 were crammed in. The prisoners in charge of the hut had the two bays nearest the door. The two bays at the other end had toilet holes dug in them.

Each remaining bay had four sets of three-tiered bunks or three sleeping shelves, one above the other, covered in paper mattresses, which were stuffed with wood shavings. With either arrangement, there would be at least fifteen people in each bay designed to hold three horses.

Prisoners still crowded this wooden hut when the camp was liberated by the **Soviet** army in January 1945.

Wooden huts in Birkenau BII had been built to be stables.

This is the inside of one of wooden huts today. The rings for the horses can be seen on the crosspiece one-third of the way up the side walls.

The wooden huts in Birkenau BII had stoves at either end to keep the huts warm, although this does not mean that they were lit regularly. Even when lit, they would not have given out a great deal of heat. The smoke from these stoves was carried along the brick **flues** that ran down the middle of the hut, to the chimney at the opposite end.

Holes were made in the flues at regular intervals to allow some warmth to escape. This also meant that smoke escaped into the hut as well.

17

Health and Hygiene

People in Birkenau BII used open **toilet pits** when the huts were first built. Then toilet and shower huts were built. The use of the toilets was restricted, as in Auschwitz I, usually to first thing in the morning and last thing at night for a very short time. There was no toilet paper, nor were there any hand-washing facilities. Many prisoners had diarrhea from too little food, and these **unhygienic** conditions made matters worse.

Keeping clean

Washing was a real problem. Birkenau was on damp, marshy ground, but there was very little fresh water, and washing facilities were almost nonexistent. People were not often allowed to use the showers that had been built. When they did, all the occupants of a block had to shower at once. They had to take off their clothes at their **barracks** and then run, naked—even in deep winter snow—to the shower block. This was often the last straw for the sick—it could kill them.

These toilets were left when the wooden huts of Birkenau were torn down. There were three rows of seats, with about 130 holes to each row.

Each **compound** of Birkenau BII had its own kitchen, which was the only building with fresh running water. The food was cooked there and then taken to each hut and distributed by the **Blockältester**. **Rations** were the same as those in Auschwitz I.

Prisoners at Auschwitz were badly undernourished, often starving to death. This meant they had almost constant diarrhea and pus-filled boils and were often feverish. What happened when they caught other infections or hurt themselves while working? There were doctors among the prisoners who tried to help as much as they could. It was important for the prisoners to stay as healthy as possible, so that they looked capable of work. If they were seriously ill or injured, they would be either sent to the **gas chambers** to be killed—selections were held regularly to weed out the sick—or taken to the hospital block. More often than not, they were not treated in the hospital block, but were used for medical experiments.

The kitchen blocks for each section of Birkenau BII were at the same end of each compound. Now only some of the brick chimneys remain.

Birkenau BI: Brick Huts

The brick huts in Birkenau BI were put up quickly, with no foundations. The floors were just mud at first, but later some were covered with concrete or brick. There were two stoves with a shared chimney for each side of the hut, but they were seldom lit. There were seventeen windows, which were barred shut on the outside, and two vents in the roof. The vents were the only way to get air because the doors were kept shut.

Prisoners slept on sleeping shelves. Sometimes they were given straw to put between themselves and the bare planks. At least four people slept on each shelf. When a new transport arrived, the huts were even more crowded—up to fifteen people were fitted on to a single shelf. So many people, even at starvation **rations,** could break the planks.

Here is one of the brick huts in Birkenau BI.

The sleeping shelves of the brick huts were airless.

PLAN: Birkenau, brick huts

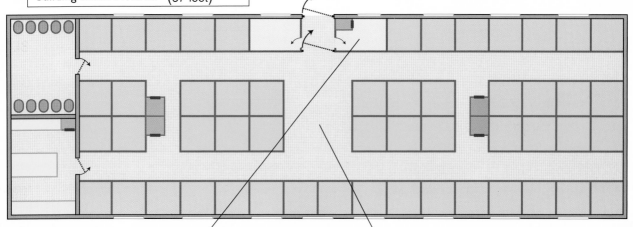

⤴ doorways, with direction of opening

◻ sleeping space, three tiers, shelves

◻ Blockältester's room and bread store

◼ stoves ◻ sinks

◯◯ toilets ⬚ windows

building height 5.80 m	(19 feet)
building length 36.25 m	(119 feet)
building width 11.40 m	(37 feet)

Stoves were built at each point marked with a purple square on the plan.

The **Blockältester** had his own room, with a stove, by the entrance.

The central assembly area was often decorated with slogans. The big sign over the door says "Cleanliness is your duty!" The smaller signs on each side of the door say "Don't drink the water, it carries contagious disease!"

Keeping Clean

Although Birkenau BI had brick kitchens, toilets, washrooms, and shower blocks, the food was the same as in other parts of Auschwitz. The showers were used as infrequently as those in BII. The use of washing facilities was also as restricted as in the rest of the camp.

Prisoners in all parts of Auschwitz were infested with fleas and lice, which could spread easily around the incredibly cramped sleeping areas. Their clothes were disinfected from time to time, and the prisoners were, too. They were dunked in tubs full of water with chemicals such as **chlorine** added, which could burn their eyes and throats just from inhaling the vapor. If they refused to go right under the water, they were pushed under and held down, sometimes until they drowned.

Here is a kitchen block for a BI **compound.**

This is a shower block for a BI compound. Prisoners were herded across the grounds naked to the showers, as in BII.

In this washroom of a BI compound, there are places for the soap, but soap was not always available. If there was soap, it was a mixture of fat and ash that did not foam properly, making it hard to wash with.

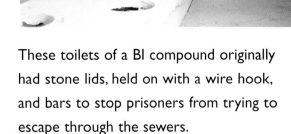

These toilets of a BI compound originally had stone lids, held on with a wire hook, and bars to stop prisoners from trying to escape through the sewers.

Misleading impressions

Many of the huts in Birkenau BI had their own washrooms and toilets at one end of the hut, in two facing sleeping spaces. Each of these was shut off from the rest of the hut by a door, and the washroom had its own stove. Each toilet block had eight china toilets, as used in Auschwitz I. Although this does not seem like a lot for 700 or more people, it still seems like an attempt on the part of the **Nazis** to make living conditions more bearable.

In fact, work on the washrooms and toilets did not begin until mid-1944. Rather than a genuine attempt to make life better for the prisoners, this late start looks like an attempt to cover up how bad conditions had been. The washrooms and toilets were never connected to the water, drains, or sewers and were never used. All they did was cut down the amount of room for sleeping by taking away eight shelves.

These washrooms and toilets were never used.

Invisible People

So far, we have examined how people lived in Auschwitz. From 1942 onward, more and more trainloads of people passed through Auschwitz without being recorded. Jewish people, especially, were sent straight to their deaths. As the German army took over more countries, Jews from those countries were shipped directly to Auschwitz-Birkenau.

The Jews' journey could take many days, all without food or water, and with just one small bucket—or nothing—to use as a toilet. Many people died on the journey. Those who survived to reach Birkenau could pass through the camp to their deaths in a matter of hours. They left no trace behind them but the growing piles of their possessions, which filled 30 huts in a special **compound** in Birkenau BII. These possessions, ranging from clothes and hairbrushes to the hair shaved from prisoners's heads, were kept for reuse. The **Nazis** were obsessed with getting as much profit from their prisoners as possible.

The huge mound of suitcases in the Auschwitz State Museum shows that the people who owned them came from all over Europe. Just this small part of the pile shows that people came from countries as far apart as Holland and Greece.

The Nazis blew up the **crematoria** at Auschwitz, where they burned the bodies of their victims, as soon as they realized the **Soviets** were advancing on the camp. They did not do a good enough job of destruction. There is still enough left to work out what the buildings were used for. The metal tracks visible here were for the carts used to slide the bodies into the ovens.

Crematorium I at Auschwitz I has been reconstructed so that visitors can see what would have happened there.

Victims going into a **gas chamber** (below) were told this was a shower room, where they would be able to wash after their long journey.

The rear of the crematorium (above)

The walls and doors were thick, and there was a strong system of locks on a gas chamber.

The dead were then loaded, several at a time, onto carts, wheeled to the ovens, and burned (below).

Zyklon B crystals, which produced a deadly gas, were poured into the chamber through holes in the roof.

How Many People?

How many people went straight to their deaths? The simple answer is that we do not know, not even to the nearest million people. The latest research suggests that at least one and a half million unregistered people, most of them Jewish, were killed at Auschwitz. Some historians have estimated the number at closer to four million.

The **Nazis** withdrew from Auschwitz in a hurry. They blew up the **crematoria** at Birkenau and set fire to the huts filled with the possessions of those they had murdered. They also began to burn their records at Birkenau and Auschwitz I. But they did not have time to completely destroy the evidence. The camps were too big and the **Soviet** army arrived sooner than expected. So there is some evidence left. This evidence, and the **testimonies** of survivors, go some way to showing the extent of the terrible crime that was committed at Auschwitz.

Here are some of the millions of Zyklon B canisters found at Birkenau. The contents of these canisters were used in the **gas chambers** of Auschwitz.

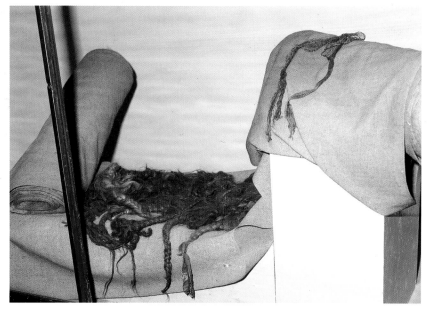

This is one of the many bolts of cloth that were scientifically analyzed and found to have been made from human hair, probably female hair. When the camp was liberated, seven tons of hair ready to be sold to make cloth or stuff mattresses were found.

Evidence of the crime

The Auschwitz State Museum has huge piles of belongings that were not burned before the Soviet army arrived. These, just a small part of the possessions put into storage, show that the Nazis killed young and old, male and female. Auschwitz was one of many camps. The site emphasizes the huge scale of the Nazi operations. The belongings are reminders that each one of those millions of people was not a number or a **statistic,** but a person, just like you.

Timeline

1933	(Jan.) **Nazi** party comes to power. Hitler becomes Chancellor, or leader, of Germany.
1935	Racist Nuremberg Laws passed in Germany discriminate against Jews, by, for example, forbidding marriages between Jews and non-Jews.
1939	(Sept. 3) Britain and France declare war after Germany invades Poland, starting World War II.
1940	Auschwitz I set up.
1941	Birkenau set up. A decision is made to establish death camps for the killing of Jews. (Sept.) First mass **gassings** take place at Auschwitz I. (Nov. 11) Germany invades USSR.
1945	(Jan.) **Soviet** army nears Auschwitz. **SS** soldiers begin to destroy **crematoria** and other evidence of mass murder. (Jan. 18) Auschwitz liberated by Soviet army.

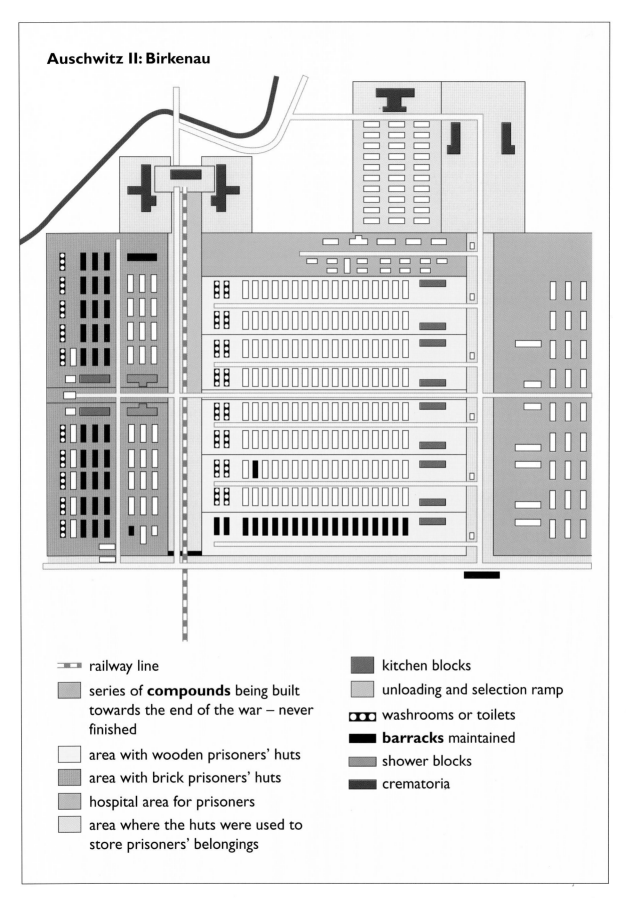

Auschwitz II: Birkenau

railway line

series of **compounds** being built towards the end of the war – never finished

area with wooden prisoners' huts

area with brick prisoners' huts

hospital area for prisoners

area where the huts were used to store prisoners' belongings

kitchen blocks

unloading and selection ramp

washrooms or toilets

barracks maintained

shower blocks

crematoria

Glossary

Aryan those whom the Nazis believed belonged to the German "master race," with characteristics such as blonde hair and blue eyes.

barracks large buildings used to house groups of soldiers

Blockältester prisoner in charge of a block or barrack at Auschwitz

calorie unit used to measure the energy value of food

chlorine gas that, when added to water, produces a solution that bleaches things and, if it is a strong solution, can burn the skin

compound area containing buildings surrounded by a fence or wall

concentration camp camp created by the Nazis for the imprisonment of people who they thought were "undesirable," such as communists, homosexuals, or Jews. Many of these camps became death camps, dedicated to the extermination of prisoners, especially Jews, in what became known as the Final Solution.

crematorium place where human bodies are burned

flue channel for carrying heat from a stove or fire

gas chamber large, well-sealed room, with access for gas or gas-producing crystals, where many people could be gassed at once

gassing killing people by exposing them to a gas that fills their lungs and stops them from breathing

guardhouses places where guards can stand and watch over various parts of a prison camp

Nazi member of the National Socialist German Workers Party, which was led by Adolf Hitler and held power in Germany between 1933 and 1945

persecute to treat someone cruelly or unfairly

political prisoner person imprisoned for opposing the government, usually for holding different political beliefs

quarantine period of isolation for newcomers to a place, to check that they do not have any infectious diseases that they could give to the people already there

rations planned allotments of food for a group of people

resistance fighting back against an invader

rights all people have the right to certain things, such as the right to live and the right to sufficient food and shelter

roll call calling out a list of names to find out who is present

Soviet belonging to the Union of Soviet Solialist Republics (USSR), a communist state that included Russia and many smaller nations

SS abbreviation for *Schutzstaffel,* or Lightning Guard, Hitler's personal guards, who were also responsible for overseeing death camps

statistics facts and figures

testimony any statement or evidence, such as that given in a court of law or by survivors of Nazi death camps

toilet pit hole dug in the ground, usually outside, to use as a toilet

unemployment not having work

unhygienic not clean and healthy

More Books to Read

Ayer , Eleanor H. and Stephen D. Chicoine. *From the Ashes: May 1945 & After.* Woodbridge, Conn.: Blackbirch, 1997.

Gottfried, Ted. *The Holocaust & Nazi Germany.* Springfield, N. J.: Enslow Publishers, 1998.

Lace, William W. *The Death Camps.* San Diego: Lucent Books, 1997.

Nieuwsma, Milton J. *Kinderlager: An Oral History of Young Holocaust Survivors.* New York: Holiday House, 1998.

Rice, Earle. *The Final Solution.* San Diego: Lucent Books, 1997.

*I*ndex